BEWITCHED
PLAYGROUND

Other Books by David Rivard

Wise Poison
Torque

BEWITCHED

PLAYGROUND

DAVID RIVARD

GRAYWOLF PRESS

Saint Paul, Minnesota

Publication of this volume is made possible in part by a grant provided by the Minnesota State Arts Board through an appropriation by the Minnesota State Legislature, and by a grant from the National Endowment for the Arts. Significant support has also been provided by the Bush Foundation; Dayton's, Mervyn's, and Target stores through the Dayton Hudson Foundation; the McKnight Foundation; and other generous contributions from foundations, corporations, and individuals. To these organizations and individuals we offer our heartfelt thanks.

Published by Graywolf Press
2402 University Avenue, Suite 203
Saint Paul, Minnesota 55114
All rights reserved.

www.graywolfpress.org

Published in the United States of America

ISBN 1-55597-302-7

2 4 6 8 9 7 5 3 1
First Graywolf Printing, 2000

Library of Congress Catalog Card Number: 99-067239

Cover Design and Illustration by Michaela Sullivan

Acknowledgments

Grateful acknowledgment is made to the editors of the following publications in which the poems, sometimes in different versions, first appeared:

AGNI: "My Education on Earth," "Question for the Office of Recycling," "Question for the Magic Hour," "Versace"
Alaska Quarterly Review: "Voice-Over"
American Poetry Review: "Clarity?," "Hello, Traveler," "Jung"
The Boston Book Review: "Golden Year," "Question for a Match Whose Flame Is Ascension," "Daydream"
Boston Phoenix: "Friend"
The Boston Review: "Question for the Bride"
Green Mountains Review: "Lucky Slaves," "Nightly"
The Greensboro Review: "Question for the Student," "A Dream"
Harvard Review: "Bewitched Playground," "Guests of the Wedding," "Not Guilty"
Lingo: "Question for the Teacher"
Mid-American Review: "Going"
Ploughshares: "America"
Provincetown Arts: "Speech to Be Made by X in the Next Life, Whenever He Gets the Chance"
Slate: "What I Know," "The Favored," "Docudrama"
Third Coast: "Anger"
Tikkun: "Temptation"
Verse: "January 30, 1994"

My thanks to Dean Young, Stuart Dischell, David Guenette, Mark Cox, Rick Jackson, David Wojahn, Candice Reffe, Stratis Haviaras, Gail Mazur, Peter Richards, David Daniel, Robert Pinsky, Steve Cramer, Tom Perrotta, Ales Debeljak, Tomaz Salamun, Fred Marchant, Fiona McCrae, and Michaela Sullivan (as per always).

Linda Bamber, Tony Hoagland, and Tom Sleigh read these poems as they were being written, as well as an early version of the book—their comments and support were a great help.

The epigraph is taken from "For a Stone Girl at Sanchi" by Gary Snyder, from *The Black Country,* copyright ©1968 by Gary Snyder. Reprinted by permission of New Directions Publishing Corp.

Part of the lyrics by Bob Dylan in "America" are from "It Takes a Lot to Laugh, It Takes a Train to Cry" and "Visions of Johanna" copyright © 1965, by Warner Bros. Music, copyright renewed 1993 by Special Rider Music. All rights reserved. International copyright secured. Reprinted by permission.

Contents

for Simone,
for Barbara & Norman

touching,
this dream pops. it was real:
and it lasted forever.

—Gary Snyder

My Cliff

My cliff, my cliffside, my oceanside
            cliff.

      Like everything else mine—

I don't own it,
      I walk around outside its life,
or else lean there;
         if need be
on occasion I lie atop it
      (after asking permission first!)—

always on the outside

      but face & belly to the sky,
        I lie down

where I can be swept by warm rain
      that has crossed water
deep & so wide
      I cannot get over alone.

Guests of the Wedding

Does it ever end? Sure, hard to say where tho, & naturally
the facts of the next thirty minutes or years
are not like tent pegs pounded into the earth,
not knowable because sharp & stationary.
But that morning walking beneath the tent—
a large tent—I saw
there was candlewax pooled on the starched white tablecloths,
proof of the pleasure
people had taken
circling & dancing & burning in the light
those candles threw the night before.
Thank you, gracious candles.
It was a wedding.
All of us, Michaela said, are really
animals, & she accepted that, glad.
And that morning
in the house belonging to Candice & Ed
next to the tent we met
the boy named Jake, a four-year-old, & his mother
with her tattoo designed by an unknown hand
to encircle like a wide bracelet her tanned upper arm,
a bracelet marked by totemic shapes & faces—
beaks, fins, talons, feathered tails, lidded eyes—
Kwakiutl if there were no Kwakiutl around to ask
the mother of Jake why & from where & who
did she think she was? Who was she
who had also had drawn across her back
shoulder blade to blade an unfurled pair of wings?
She was a lovely citizen & an employee of Ed
if the obvious can be counted on
sometimes in the sharp late-September sunlight.
Many things might happen to her

but those tattoos remain the same
or changed only slightly of course
by the fading of color,
slackened skin. Many things
would happen, her future—
months without jobs, & later,
success, against a backdrop of stables, success,
and then the night she would nearly be raped,
the rainy night she would fish
the beach with Brazilians, & on another shore
the morning she'd lick a pebble & laugh
to tell her as-yet-unborn daughter
I am Demosthenes & must practice my oration—
the future I invented for her,
and within which
I moved her from place to place.
To own another person, completely, in the imagination.
How else do you teach yourself
what you wish to become?
And isn't it
one after another after another after another
the many things men & women wish to be?

America

If it is late Sunday in the brain & sunlight
falling on the wall of the Food Court
and you tell me your daughter
at 18 months still breast-feeds,
and if I with my slightly younger daughter
sitting at the next table nod but say nothing, nothing,
while you speak of the vicissitudes
of cracked nipples & late-night feedings,
then I am someone who is
you can tell yourself
an odd man, dumb, & probably weird,
weird, weird enough
to see in the baffling dear creature you are
a classical subject for a civilized poet in an innocent land,
such as ours would be.
In that poem you would still be a woman
but made-out now as a beautiful thinly tall broomstick,
pale but not at all bony,
with encircling copper necklace & threaded red sash.

I have a devil, I own a devil,
my devil,
and he'd defend whoever sang.

So all right,
I am strange—a usually shameful matter
for an American—& would make myself even more so
to you
by revealing a secret from my life.
It's something.
I watched my wife feed our girl the milk
as both seemed to sleep those minutes
until the baby stopped, started crying,

and I took her downstairs & walked
back & forth on the planked oak floor.
It was 3:31 A.M.,
and I put the music on low
only to initiate my daughter
into the religion of Bob Dylan.
Well I ride on a mail train, baby, can't buy a thrill.
Ain't it just like the night, to play tricks
when you're trying to be so quiet.

I want you to know these things.

So what are you waiting for?

Go ahead, ask.

Don't hold your breath
if you want to breathe,
my beautiful broom.

Bewitched Playground

Each could picture probably
with great care his brother drawing
the corded string of a watered silk bag
and mumbling to Basho above the keepsake
pay your respects to mother's white hair
now your eyebrows look a little white too
but all have turned instead to watch this child
a girl my daughter Simone
an astute migrant
skimming the stream of days
toted wherever she wants
to eat the dirt of inattentive towns
to arm wrestle as with
the blind & steal a stoic
shipping him home—
all have turned & run to her because
she has a spider on her neck she has
seen herself
though blindfolded by a cloud
the sun is a yellowjacket
drowning in a cup of coffee she carries
a spider in her hair
blond & blonder dear river.

Temptation

Tho we sit there smiling with wet hair
in green grass & broad daylight

nonetheless silently we must
as a requirement agree to die.

That is it, the worst
of the whole

silly business—
that is the worst thing

they fear, those blessed
melancholiacs who shudder among us,

who should love properly
our springs, & summers,

plush summer—pollinated
dahlias, unbuttoned pajama

tops, zinc oxide
at all the lifeguard shacks—

      love this, I say
      come on,

but they can't & don't.
They won't

be tempted to be
ordinary.

They are the ones & they are
the only—trying to wait it out.

My Education on Earth

It's not snowing but it snows
the dry defiant powder
wind spills off roofs like a blizzard
of feedback from a guitar,
a cheap Sears special tuned by a god
who dreams himself
trapped somehow
within the body of a stoned
and temporarily
unemployed auto worker.
As for me, I too
need to be woken. I would like
to be woken
conclusively—if necessary, by
burning embers—so that I might begin
my education on earth.
Only I'm worried
I've planted
the bulbs improperly.
After all
in six to eight weeks
they are supposed to become a gift
everyone would want—those tulips—
their yellow, persistent
and unsighing—unless
they have been planted badly,
upside down for instance.
In which case the directions
seem to imply
there will be no warm rains to sweep the streets,
no spring showers like gold coins falling

headfirst
against the earth's trampoline.
And when I shuck my shirts
at night they will still give
off sparks in the dark,
cold air sucking life
from the collars & cuffs. So—
the day may have been dug badly,
growing downward now
apparently forever.
But I annoy myself to be
so sensitive—
it makes me
sleepy! I am asleep
in a week some calendars call
the week of March 1st, & in need
like the steam
as it rises swirling & distracted
into cold daylight
out of a dryer full of
wet hot clothes.
Steam, I say, *smarten up—*
get over it.

What I Know

I don't know the happiness felt
by that woman who believes
she can actually
recall being a cold bullet
fallen in a field of trampled spring clover
without having hit anyone
lying there dead or groaning.

Neither can I know the happiness
of the one man among us
who remembers so clearly
his life long ago
as that aspiring but naive piece of parchment
on which a tribe of mistrustful lords
and barons
wrote the Magna Carta.

But because the steam-heated
winter dries
Simone's skin I know
I get to stand by the still-warm tub filled
with bath toys—

> toothless killer whale
> reborn
> as cruise missile,
> two turtles (mind readers),
> one pirated galleon beached
> atop the styrofoam
> hyacinth, & floating facedown
> in the water (abandoned,
> lonely as a double-crossed bagman)
> the begoggled action Barbie

manufactured nude
in either Hwangshih
or Kowloon;

and pouring oil into
my cupped palm
I get to lift her hair
so as to rub the oil over back, blonded
swirls along her neck, coarse
scraped elbow, thighs,
and this
is the happiness—
I know
happiness
squealing.

Question for the Student

No rose deludes itself by thinking
it knows the truth,

no beagle daydreams
of being a fearsome wolf,

no rock of mating with a deer;

and out of the blowsy
pink hydrangea
swayed by a veranda breeze

comes a scent
it cannot smell—

darling,
daring one,

aren't those flowers lucky?

Daydream

Wishes need
people,
constantly, & so

as he sits there (among friends)
with the day
starting to feel like a heavy bag—

a big supermarket brown sack
crammed with letters,
angry letters—he pretends

he can call on his father
(unshaven, long-dead) to haul them all
away. The letters accuse him,

of not being
what he wanted & being what he is.
His father could take them

wherever it is the dead lug
whatever they are asked—
in this case a canal town

south in France—
midge-fazed water, barge boats,
a café deck of teak,

because he dreams often
of this place.
Above the village

an upland vineyard.
The vines have thrived
for years, but lately

mists on the hillsides
hold hostage some nights,
cold, worrisome

nights, survivable
for sure now
only by burning

(as he pictures his father doing)
one of those letters
each hour, its flame carried

back & forth through
the terraced rows,
one slow-burning letter

per hour
of all those his father sent him
while alive.

Anger

For a long time it would happen whenever
paging through a book I felt betrayed—
say by an almanac of birds,
if it suggested a heaven
where judgment might be rendered
exclusively
according to the elegance of song
and supremacy of feather.

Or when I leaned forward
those rainy summer evenings to hear
how the wind
with its sluicing & sleep-rattling
put into my ear the nearly noiseless slice of fins—
what others would call a whistle,
the whistle of conquerors & rich officials—
the slice of fins
cutting a passage across smooth blue water,
bringing me their hellos.

Whenever I leaned like that,
it happened.

Happened
whenever I felt most myself,
when words,
their failures waving farewell,
selected me as the one who would put down
the thing many others had also heard Hagler say
in Provincetown
in 1984 by an indoor swimming pool in a hotel
where from the walls surrounding
his training-camp boxing ring

we were all eyed
by the untethered & absurdly optimistic depictions,
the nearly adolescent shyness,
the ghost-insulting smiles
of the Pilgrims John & Priscilla Alden—
those murals of them
embodying an uncomplicated innocence,
though they had crossed an ocean, an ocean,
their longings rosy & blurred,
soapy,
obviously & contemptuously unlike
my own or Marvin Hagler's, nickname Marvelous,
then the middleweight title-holder,
now an actor in spaghetti westerns
and network deodorant commercials.

It happened.

It happened
when he jabbed, bobbed, & to no one
in particular said
if they cut my bald head open
all they'll find is one big boxing glove.

And it happened & would happen
and for a long time
each time
I believed in some things:

my anger,

and whatever it was
I thought I hated.

Nightly

Nightly in sleep those usually
as meek as Raggedy Ann
gobble up whole
the still steaming heads of their dead enemies—

the meek are God's
armed & most dangerous & swift hunters,

their secret hardness shall not be soothed.

If I had a peaceful heart
I would be as cruel as they are.

Home

Forced to say what living feels like.

And then
forced to act out that feeling
at dusk I pull on the jumpsuit
my meter-reader wears
and stand in a field of fresh-mown hay,
swaying, & measuring the stunned electricity
grasshoppers transmit
while searching for a home.

To feel at home. To find one.

It seems always
just about
to open, unlocked
by something small as the taste say
of piped-in 20th-century water.
Then it goes. The glass empties, & takes
the moment with it. The moment
goes, constantly.

Thoughtlessly. Faithfully.

It was a moment like this
that the Mormons showed up once at my door,
having pumped hard
on their bicycle pedals.

Lo & Behold!

Skinny-legged, & wearing those
shiny black nameplates. These Mormons,
they're brave—
so certain of who

they are & where they belong,
with names that look eternal
on any buttoned-down white oxford shirt.

I trembled before them,
as an ant might
before a massed planting of peonies.

If I had licked them, their terrible
feeble Elders would have keeled over,
struck down—by horror,
or (who knows?)
joy.

Lo & Behold, Lo & Behold.

Question for the Magic Hour

Out of pocket & just before dark
the wind simpers into town—tired,
and a little annoyed,
after having stewed for such
a long, long time
in its own bittersweet schemes
and choices.

A wind that's
distracted, & vague,
sniffly—
like a rabbit, or a sedated professor.

It should come instead
like a helpful devil or deadly god
this wind.

This wind should carry the horny
summer smell of pine needles,
such as those
a boatload of nippled sleepers might breathe
if anchored not
too far from shore.

Or else it should wander out of
that alley
back of the crossroad tavern
my witchy sister-in-law once owned,
the alley paved with pissed-on brick
and crud
spilled from dumpsters,
a breeze fed by the dreamless constant
roar of fryolator vents.

Like a deadly god, or a helpful devil—
let the wind come like
either of these, & fit
to be
tied, all right?

I plan to hug it & hide it from my neighbors.

for Mary Ruefle

Versace

Perfume off the pages of a magazine   inexplicable
vendettas   pollen   of beach grass   from beachtowns
the constant talk of weapons   American   American
sins   & ads for antihistamines   all this

      was the wind's news, especially

poor Versace: neither plug-ugly
      nor a looker, himself,

of all the day's dead guys   the tastiest   & most
   tasteless,
   who'd gone out
fishing for his morning
newspaper;

whatever new fashion he has taken up

(now that the old is abandoned,

that style the spiders call
running-back-&-forth-inside-ourselves,
as they themselves run,
inside silk wisps
spun from their bellies)

whatever new fashion has taken him up—

fine, fine!

Jung

Sitting down at age eighty-one to record his life
Jung made no mention of the fin de siècle
Swiss bath or the fifteen-year-old boy he had been
long ago standing there in a mirror & watching
as he stepped carefully into the underpants of a girl.
Slipping them over his thighs—nervous, but
not rushing, attentive. The girl his blond cousin.
Jung wrote nothing of this, he told no one.
Though about the evening a long carving knife
snapped itself into four more or less equal pieces
he managed ten pages describing & interpreting
how as it lay untouched in an oaken sideboard
the scratched steel blade shattered with a loud bang.
Whatever force broke it caused him also to abandon
his medical studies & start to survey the psyche.
He believed this & could report it straight-faced,
fervent, but told no one of the other earlier
scene—his ears bee-stung, his chest a riptide
of the silk of his cousin's pants rubbing against
his penis, his balls, touching the tightening coarse
sparse hairs alert to the cloth. In his book
he gives away almost all his secrets. That he
was required toward the end of his life to do so,
this was one source of his power, his healing
of the untuned unstrung souls who came freely
or by reference & authority were ferried to him—
the murderess, the catatonic rug-maker, paranoids,
an impotent wine merchant, the city planner,
a fearful Jesuit, scribbler of puns—those
filled with silence or willing to say anything,
like *I am Socrates, the unjustly accused,*
I am the double polytechnic irreplaceable,

Naples & I must supply the world with noodles.
He healed because he was filled by secrets
he understood he must eventually give up,
all but one. That was the bargain, a covenant.
But between being empty or being full
what difference is there, & what gondola
shuttles us from one shore to the other?
What if no difference exists, though Jung lived
as if it did? His mother walked into the bathroom
unexpectedly, they looked at each other & she
removed herself shutting the door quietly. About
the incident neither said a word to the other.
Jung carried the pieces of the shattered knife
the rest of his life & each time he moved carefully
put the four pieces of blade in the top drawer
of his desk, in the corners, the four directions wind
blows from, the names of which are only names.

A Dream

The thing is, it so happened—
trust me it's true—but the thing is
there was a lamp I threw,

I lobbed it out the window,

along with as much
of the other furniture as
possible—something Victorian first,
a Morris chair, & then
the modern stuff, a modem, a wall safe,
even the tinfoil & family photos—
everything
except for those crumbs
preferred by the house's rats, & which
no connoisseur wishes to eat.

Except for us then the house
would be empty
of the many things we own
(that was the point of the dream)—

it's a way
for us to change,
you said,

a spell:

endless need, envy,

in lieu of calm & satisfaction.

No, I said, not envy,

it's flawed,
it wouldn't be useful.

Still, you said, it's a
tragic flaw—

if we only
had a tragic flaw, our shadows
could converse with those
of Achilles & Lady Macbeth.

And then someone
standing near us said

Oh, you mean
those people the gods call
shoppers.

Question for the Bride

Now that everything seems so persuasive
you will go on changing   as always
it has always been the case with you
whether you knew it or not   ever since
that morning in the swamp   that Sunday
a sunless windy morning   when
right in front of you   a fat hive dropped
unbidden   out of a blackened tree
a tupelo   and where it fell   the water
was shallow   eighteen inches at most
but in it   one hundred & fifty-six wasps
drowned   so   no   you are not
finished   your apprenticeship is not yet over
you have fallen in love   inadvertently   you
are the bride-to-be   and now   having
dressed yourself in the gown   for practice
you must stand before a mirror
in the upper right-hand corner of
which   all of a sudden   a courtroom
will appear   the litigants judge & jury
suspended there   in midair   a news
bulletin   the reporter's face reflected
from a portable television far across
the room   the sound turned down
the litigants looking tense   or bored
the whole crew of them a little
self-conscious   like characters who have
just recently been conjured   though somewhat
incompletely   by a staff of studio writers
in Century City   California
In a field off a Vermont road   later
this week   you'll listen to a car ticking

as it cools   the sound of the engine
blending with the cicadas in tall bluegrass
floating past   as in a dream then
you will finger the veil & lift
your mother & father long ago set aside
in a folder for silences & song
you'll waken   almost immediately
reborn   you will have lifted the veil
though of course   sooner or later   farther
down the line   that stranger   the one
with whom you spend so much time
in your mind   talking   he will reveal
he is your brother   and what
will you have to say to him then   when
as he must   he asks if you had
allowed yourself to lead a happy life
in spite of the fact your parents
had not   what is it you will tell him
what answer can you give?

Not Guilty

The days are dog-eared, the edges torn,
ragged—like those pages
I ripped once out of library books,

for their photos
of Vallejo and bootless Robert Johnson.
A fine needs paying now

it's true, but
not by me.
I am no more guilty

than that thrush is
who sits there stripping moss
off the wet bark of a tree.

A red fleck, like his, glows
at the back of my head—a beauty mark,
left by the brain's after-jets.

I would not wish for the three brains
Robert required
to double-clutch his guitar

and chase those sounds he had to know
led down
and into a troubled dusky river, always.

Three brains did Johnson no earthly good,
neither his nor Vallejo's 4 & ½
worked right exactly—O bunglers,

O banged-up pans of disaster!
Crying for days, said Cesar, & singing for months.
How can I be so strong some times,

at others weak? I wish to be free,
but free to do what? To leave myself behind?
To switch channels remotely?

Better to sing.
Not like the bird, but as they sang,
Cesar & Robert—

with the shocked & seeded
sweetness of an apple
split open by a meat cleaver.

Nice Work If You Can Get It

Spending her days oh yeah waking in my head
this woman (in a short skirt,
of black stretched jersey). Her hair bright

and whipping across my lips, a wry
sort of wild. She has me
dancing, a little dirty again

on this floating veranda of a life.
Her with her charming back to me, & lightly,
snug, brushing her lovely butt

against me, & here, as my fingertips did once
I like to
trace, lingering clumsily, touching

the damp skin above her hip
as the black skirt rides low,
before homing down her thigh.

Autobiographically speaking,
I didn't mind being awkward, nervous
a little, it felt good.

Feels good.
I want my tongue there.
Tasting the flavor. Salt.

But this is for trouble only—
testing everything. Tongue, must you
lick the tiny wildering hairs

blonding her belly? Why not turn
your attentions
sanely, even if sullen, elsewhere,

over there, toward that silvered pair
of cold cuff links? How about
the peppercorn, or Nordic felt?

I could change her life forever.

Docudrama

Finally, the night did
what night always does, it swallowed
my two friends, their arms
slung around each other's waists as I drove off
chasing my high beams.
Outside their shingled walls & roof
and surrounded by pinewoods
a few minutes earlier that evening
my friends & I had been saying good-bye
when one of them, the man—
surprised by the baby seat suddenly visible
in the back of the car (lit up by an interior light
as I opened the door)—he said, my friend
said *Jeez,*
they (meaning Michaela & our daughter Simone),
they won't be able to go anywhere.
Seeing I was as far as 150 miles from home
with the car, & my being
a potential traffic fatality,
or worse (deadbeat dad, abandoner), he was right.
I saw myself a moment
as indispensable, happy to be needed, much like
a canoe-paddling guide or gondola pilot.
But my other friend—
the woman—squinting at the baby seat
with pity & amusement, she said *For christ's sake,*
you might as well wear a chastity belt.
And somehow
the mention of sex dragged death behind it—
I mean
now that I have settled
(with responsibilities)

my dates with this or that sexual tsunami should
be a thing of the past,
right?
So there I was—caught
between being one man or another, neither.
Really, none of this is tragic.
Can I be loved enough? that's my story.

To My Wife

The bumper sticker says it out straight—"Vegetarians Taste Good."
I am only a starving sacred cow, love, but I beg to undress for you.

Birthmark

Under orders not exactly
our own it appears

each of us—man & woman—
is sent off at birth
into a life entirely ours.

For some,
the windless haze of humid vineyards
(farm camps, migrant labor);

for others, heedless
coasting, the heedlessness
of hang gliding

or carjackings—

wouldn't that be a life?

—

Somewhere—perhaps
within the pages of some
stinking leather-bound book
(maroon in color)—it may be
that a few lines of cramped
handwriting have arranged
for my dearest friend's existence
to feel just like a day in the
life of a thistle, a shaft
of highway pig-straw.

—

As for his sister (my wife),

that birthmark which she hates

because it covers half
the top of her quick left hand

is (among
many other features) a thing
I love,

since it
makes it easier
to follow

while she runs a
thin white string
through the hole
dead center
of three
dozen or so
Cheerios,

a string meant to be
dangled all day
from our daughter's neck—

(amulet!)

January 30, 1994

What is man that thou art mindful of him?

He can play a guitar he calls Blackbird by name.
He could talk a dog off a meat wagon, you bet.

A Kidnapping, Some Mook Might Say

of that day in the museum
when she was four (or maybe five),
tho it was actually

her father
lifting her to look at a mask
the Tsimishian called

The Watcher for Guests in the Grass—
this mask
that seemed to be the one

talking, because she heard it,
it said *go ahead*
it's alright   it's good   you'll like it,

and so she had, she
had let herself run her fingers then
through fur hide sewn

into heavy winter robes
by the men & women of
fogged-in settlements

long-gone, she'd bent down
as her father urged her
to brush her nose & lips against

the kelp-cool hairs of an otter pelt,
and felt herself
being tugged, taken, whisked away—

by ghosts—not kidnapped,
but lifted, as a vein-red maple leaf might be
in an unexpectedly

warm November wind,
driven over brick & slate sidewalk,
it tumbles, the leaf

somersaults onto a guitar case
carried by an unknown hand, it sticks
in the handle, caught,

until this stranger arrives
at his spot near
the automatic teller in the square,

where the leaf settles, briefly,
underneath the shredded but insistent
remains of a red & blue poster

recommending to all
who pass by
the names Mondale & Ferraro—

Going

Sunlight fades
the storefront full of magazines.
Month to month
they boss us—the covers,
they tell us
that if we want to get happy & alluring
(real happy, alluring sexually)
we must for goddamn sure
take up the breeding of Jack Russell terriers,
or else dig
ourselves
a little backyard fishpond.

Days of fish, days of dog, days of sex—
in that order, necessarily.

In the sun
all the titles are trying
to vanish—phrases like *trout pond*
diluted, the 20-point sans serif, inked-red
passion bleached now, apathetic, ghostly—
words that want my attention
like movers on the street lugging mirrors,
a moment when I seem to
come toward myself & then
I'm gone
too. I am not
a greedy man. All I want
is to be a visitor to this life.

Question for the Teacher

A big jaw, George Oppen, you had a big jaw,
lantern not quite the right term—
though about reality
we as humans can say
something as inexact as that
and still sound sure.

Anyway,
we surge out into the open,
beating our wings, & chests,
making our claims.

Birds & apes,
that's us, but still
we meet some
things,

and they are
beautiful & elegant, or harsh, humiliating—
real—met up with, & touched.

Facts.

The clink of bottles in a recycling bin.
A rat rooting under its utility-blue lid—a rat queen.
And an iridescent feather, adrift, downwind.

But it is the law, the law
of the State of Massachusetts,
that prevents anyone
other than the crematory or funeral-home workers
from being the last
to touch a body. Thus it is
no one we know will say good-bye to us,
by touch.

George Oppen, what have you to teach me?

Nothing!—

I say it
as you said it
is

"impossible to doubt the world: it can be seen
and because it is irrevocable
it cannot be understood, and I believe that fact is lethal."

Friend

I can continue breathing, while you cannot.

So, there's your perfume.

Opening the guest room two weeks after your visit,
one week past the car crash,
and, naturally, there's your perfume—
still rehearsing its sandalwood
beside the futon & piled bedding, beside
the bottle of Poland Spring, full,
and the paper bag,
folded, left behind.

As for the bottle, I will never drink from it.
I have my superstitions.

Alive, you had yours, & no clothing
but elaborate scarves & rings, & colored hair, cut
blunt at the neck, a scented neck, bad feet,
loyalty, generosity, & thus friends,
poetry, therefore a tongue,
and terror, needs—unapproachable—& therefore
remedies,
both prescribed & proscribed,

which I saw as pegs to keep your tent
from blowing down in a dark clearing,

though they were also the wind.

In your poems you flew toward transcendence—
a mistake I always thought—
though about this I sense we were both wrong.
What a pleasure to make a mistake,

having something to recover from, & to make it
again & again.

Unfolded,
the maroon paper sack might
be more important than the crash,
considering some things
much needed by humans
could be loaded into it—

a few unshucked ears of corn,
for example,
or a board game,

maybe even books,

but only those with no
lessons to teach.

I've been thinking to open this bag
and place it behind
the cypress when it rains next,

until it is torn, & of no use to anyone.

With your permission, of course.

Speech to Be Made by X
in the Next Life,
Whenever He Gets the Chance

"That slapstick you saw me as—
alcohol, & finally a stroke or two jerking
the thin threads strung at ankles,
jaw & knees—he's the one

dead. A spook. And for you, still,
puppet. Amusement,
and lesson.   Don't go home
feeling you knew me. Your part

was small, voyeur more than advisor.
An errand boy, & darkened
body I'd fidget beside
in a San Francisco cineplex.   No.

I raised my hands to my eyes
and shouted NO! to make my mind
or Kurasawa stop a head like
mine from spinning slo-mo away—

lopped off
by a malicious warlord swordsman
who had walked the countryside for years
in insect-scaled armor.

A woman's bright silks burned,
inside her timbered fortress. The head
flew across a bonfire. In the theater
I shouted

to get the thought out
of my own broken mouth, & even louder
another time, but happy then
we were watching a bunch of Forster's

Edwardians cavort in a pool,
up to their gentle assholes in Umbrian
pond lilies. A little
faggoty I bet you thought.

After I died, I re-entered the world as
something shining & silver—
maybe the steel of that warlord's sword,
a polished blade, or pond water,

sun-struck, teasing. What about
you? how are you making it
these days—is it poverty, or pleasure?
Hard to say? The question

is foolish, I know, a pinwheel
costing as much as a windmill
whoever does the wishing.   Wishes
dream us.   Why?"

Clarity?

So long as the self accuses itself
it makes itself necessary & strikes at
shadow so long as it pretends
always to be what it is not so long
as you cannot touch who you are
and it is necessary for the pieces of
your puzzle, your great lucky story,
to be shoved deep into the lint-
packed corners of a jacket pocket,
so that the anchorage is gone
from which the ships were launched,
and there are no panties on the floor,
no cotton blouse, no husband & no
mountaintop, there is no belt buckle,
and at the airport no maze of lights,
and then the gifts go, at dusk, the boots
her husband wore in the garage, the car,
and then the dusk goes, a hell
the size of an apple seed, & there is no
slow ride across the lake, no diamond,
no cut-glass cat, & no catgut
to sew the wound, no scissors
either, & no hair the blades
might hack, no earring, no beeswax,
no glasses an old man could wipe
clear, & no sneer, indelicate,
the sand vanished, the bathwater drained,
gone, the same with the chimney
in need of pointing, the pit where
they changed the oil, the house lent
for a day, it is a pain in the neck,
a pain in the ass, but there is no

headwater for the Mississippi,
and no asp, not even a bee
wearing a cocked bosun's cap,
machine gun in one hand, hammer
in the other, there be no clouds
so swift & no sun so slow, so slow,
slow, & naturally, no loneliness
to make you grateful for having had
something or someone to serve.

Hope

Hey hey, if I
say, hey, a mosquito can pull a plow, why
of course, you should, go
on, go out, find yourself one, & hitch him up,
sweetie.

Elsewise,
how will you recover,
after such a long, long childhood spent
with all those other
gods, hard & jealous gods?

Question for the Office
of Recycling

Do not, it said. *Do not recycle any*
lavatory wash papers. No dining service papers,

waxed papers, paper cups, paper plates, carbon
paper, napkins, peanut shells, salami sandwiches,

pencil shavings, plastic wrap or styrofoam.
But I took your memo, I ripped it in half.

Because maybe
a father's job demands

he destroy some words,
here & there,

to put at risk
the world. Well, then;—

does that make saving the world
always

a child's task? I only tore that scrap
to write on the backside

my daughter's words, these,
spoken at breakfast:

"And away be birds dad, blowing
careful don't they, don't they, how far?"

Paradisiac

Stammering across the ceiling that spider
takes no interest in our fighting,
and who can blame him? If I have to be

altogether lonely—never to ride
the river with you again—who cares?
Who cares if every spring the river

swells with rain? I refuse to be lonely.
I will leave like scissors from a storage case,
I'll tilt down the stairs & cut myself off.

My face refuses to be dazed—by yours
at least, & never again, I will never be stunned
again by your talent for happiness,

glad as you are wherever you are,
glad if you're backlit by roses, & glad
when the roses wilt into rats' ears.

So how can it matter if a donkey
is what you see me as, a donkey whose owner,
the priest, sits in an orchard

wearing a ragwool sweater, weeping?
We were born there, two
small people, with the usual pockets full

of dreams & guilt. I should forget you.
But each time the priest whips me home,
I forgive him. As you forgive me.

The Favored

In the dream that repeats as certain
as dusk you walk with me
again as it happens strolling by

yards of quiet or clamoring families.
Affable street, & nothing accidental
here, so it makes sense

I like the people we pass by thinking
the sunglasses I wear
mean me a blind man.

Always you grip a white secondhand paperback.
I can almost smell the spine's
cracked glue as you read

aloud. Pulp—
narrated by a foolish minor princeling
or gypsy tinker, his eyes aquamarine,

squinting through venetian shades into
the bedroom of a scullery maid/dominatrix/police detective
who offers to straddle

the plantation master/diplomat/dope dealer's head
as he lies there on the floor,
the enticements of her taffeta, spandex, musk,

and blondness
quite clear, & if he submits—one
can only hope—he will, later, pray

to be part of the various
silver-green mosses & tendrils hanging from branches
overhanging a river. In the dream

we seem the same man & woman
who each day step out onto our porch.
Ourselves. Meat & potato eaters,

but favored. We are ordinary,
glad
someone dares to tell our story.

Voice-Over

So I never got clearheaded—
and never purposeful,
I was unfit even for the kind of life
lived by those craftsmen
who cut crude birds out of
aluminum pie plates
they scavenge from dumpsters—
I was nowhere near that focused—
but it all turned out fine,
once I put on a gown & married myself
to you, my confusion.
My bafflement, my perennial
distraction—my brother
who is me if I am honest.
It happened unexpectedly one morning
as I was crossing some traffic, staking my claim
against a road full of streaming vehicles.
On the other side, while combing my hair
in honor of the progress I'd made,
I decided never again to admire
anyone who is centered & calm.
I was sixteen years old,
or seventy-five. I was not too late.
I thought of calling my friends
in other states, but they
were asleep, their pillows
like well-used boxes of matches.
In dreams we set ourselves
on fire hopeful
of changes happening.
I wanted to tell my friends
the clouds that do all the thinking

inside my head
sang to me like a choir
the Sisters of Mercy had assembled.
Now I could ask
the woods in which my mother walked
for her release.
None of my friends could tell later
how it was my hands
got dirtied, the nails blackened.
I had forgotten much myself.
But I remember how in a side yard
off a street behind the square I had just crossed
that when one of the silk shirts
standing there
tried to correct me into the right posture
all I needed to do in reply
was press a leaf against my lips.
Oh yes the poor like us
should
celebrate.
That was progress!

Question for a Match
Whose Flame Is Ascension

It took no longer
than it might for a match
to be
struck & then flipped,

a match sent flying
into a pile of
crisp dry leaves.
It was earlier tonight

it happened,
while the sky had its usual
job to do, & did—
by impersonating a woman,

one
who'd made a mess of herself
with eyeliner.
It was then that it took place,

as my friends walked on ahead
past the one dead swallow
and past the many other
dead birds I thought

lay scattered all over
the concrete boardwalk.
It was then,
when I stayed behind

to study these birds,
that their feathers changed
into the calibrated dark
brown scales of pinecones.

Does death make
as many mistakes about us
as we do about it?
For example, the temptation

to kill oneself—
how could it possibly
be the lowest common denominator
of all garages?

When I walk
along the estuary next, I hope
it is without
any of my usual errors.

Let me make
a little mystique
for myself.
On the way there,

let me open
a door, the sixty-five-
miles-per-hour
door of a car,

so as to put my face
close
to the tarmac, a day's
heat.

Lucky Slaves

In the city, meanwhile,
the tenants come home,
the subletters & co-op owners,
dwellers beneath
slate mansard roofs & heating ducts,
they arrive one
by one, that being their way,
one by hopeless
unimportant
hopeful one—slaves—
but lucky slaves,
like the last of those last few Israelites,
they who wandered sighing & distracted
over a path
the Lord of the parted Red Sea had made.
Soon the suppers
of America
will start to be prepared.
First the paring of onions,
and then the frying.
On the forehead of the city the sun
is setting, the brow
in flames, the brain doing a cool
coppery burn. But the floor
beneath our feet remains
firm. It will not
be turned
to ash.

Hello, Traveler

Bitter sadness splits each person
so high moments
of laughter
might heal us,

and vice versa—

everything fine & good
taking place as it does before or after
the worst happens—

but all the while,
in the background, nightly,
a girl sings. She sings
the song that says
she'll sleep, she'll sleep, she'll
rest at last—

this
is how we hear it
in any case,

at least we think we do.

It is true too
that for the longest time
whenever we wave hello
we beckon
like travelers aboard schooners,

until one day
the ship makes landfall,
and off we step—

each of us chooses
finally, & having chosen

becomes the thing
whose name we picked:

cute corpse
apprentice storm
enlightened *pendejo*
sacred fox
rounder
sloth
seedling
bald poet
calculating mouse
fan of Truffaut
self-made Beowulf
beautiful laundress

or pirate hero.

Before that tho
if lucky
each dreams
of shooting six blue arrows
into the sea, & crying—
crying
for how the sea
forgives those arrows
so easily.

Golden Year

We believe in so much too.

Lonely unlonely wavelets on a copper shore.

Brainwaves. The whistling we do.

Birds. In dark thick bushes.

She stands above a river, on a pier. My girl.

She turns her pockets out, & she empties.

And it begins. A new year. Don't rest, river.

DAVID RIVARD is the author of *Wise Poison,* which won the 1996 James Laughlin Award of The Academy of American Poets, and *Torque,* which won the 1987 Agnes Lynch Starrett Poetry Prize. He is the recipient of fellowships from the National Endowment for the Arts, the Massachusetts Arts Foundation, and the Fine Arts Work Center in Provincetown, and has won a Pushcart Prize. Rivard currently teaches at Tufts University and in the M.F.A. in Writing Program at Vermont College and is poetry editor at *Harvard Review.* He lives in Cambridge, Massachusetts, with his wife and daughter.

This book was designed by Donna Burch. It is set in Adobe Garamond type by Stanton Publication Services, Inc., and manufactured by Bang Printing on acid-free paper.